The Elephant

Story by
JILL COLEMAN

Pictures by
MICHAEL ATKINSON

Angus & Robertson · Publishers

It was a hot, dusty morning. The elephant was thirsty. Her skin was dry and itchy, and a cloud of insects buzzed around her head. The rest of the herd were thirsty, too, as they trudged to the water hole for a drink and a bath.

Behind the elephant plodded her two calves; one a twelve-year-old male, the other a four-year-old female. The male calf jerked his head up and down to shake off the insects which clung to the corners of his eyes. The female clutched her mother's tail for support.

Soon the elephants could see the water hole. But they were not the first to arrive.

Some zebras and a group of wildebeests were nibbling the green grass at the edge of the pool. A hippopotamus surfaced, looked around with its beady eyes and sank beneath the water. A gazelle raised her head nervously and listened. She heard the elephants approaching and bounded away.

Although she was thirsty, the elephant stopped at the edge of the water to allow the older elephants in the herd to drink before her. The leader of the herd, an old female with a broken tusk, drank first and then waddled slowly into the water.

At last the elephant's turn came. She sucked the cool water into her trunk and sprayed her back with water. The two calves did not stop to drink. They charged straight into the water, squealing with delight. As they plunged in, they splashed mud all over the leader of the herd and trampled on the pithy reeds that she was munching.

The elephant saw the calves' bad manners and sharply butted the older one with her tusks. So he swam out to the middle of the pool and played at swimming under water. He kept his trunk above the surface so he could breathe.

His sister joined the other calves who were splashing about in the shallows. They wallowed in the mud, ducking each other and squirting mud and water through their trunks.

After her bath, the elephant left her calves to play while she wandered away to feed. Stretching her trunk, she picked the tasty leaves from the tops of the trees and stuffed them into her mouth. After a while she grew too hot again and stopped to rest. She leaned against the trunk of a huge acacia tree and flapped her big ears to keep cool.

She was almost asleep, when she noticed a male elephant lumbering towards her. He was bigger than her and his skin was red with dust. He had been following the herd for some time and she had often bathed with him. Now he sensed that she was ready to mate, and would not be scared when he came close. He put the tip of his trunk into her mouth to show he was friendly. Then she did the same to him. They touched each other with their trunks, squeaking and rumbling to each other. Then they mated.

In the evening, the male wandered off and the elephant went back to the herd. Her calves were excited to see her and nuzzled her with their trunks. For a short time the sun glowed orange and the sky was streaked with colour. Then suddenly it was dark and time for the elephant to sleep. The older elephants made a circle around the calves to protect them. Then they all slept, standing up.

For the next few weeks the elephant stayed near the water hole with the rest of the herd. But as the weather grew hotter, the water hole began to dry up. It turned into a muddy bog and soon there was only dusty earth left.

All the animals were hungry. They had already nibbled the grass right down to the roots. The elephants knocked down trees to get at the topmost leaves and ripped the bark from the baobab trees to chew the spongy wood inside. Soon there was nothing left to eat. So they had to move on.

The sun blazed down and there was no rain. Rivers dried up. Plants shrivelled and died and clouds of dust blew across the plains. The elephant and her calves walked for hours every day to find food and water.

As they walked, a flock of brilliant white egrets followed them. The birds flapped about their heads, perched on their backs, and pecked the ground by their feet. The birds and the elephants were firm friends because the insects that bothered the elephants were the egrets' favourite food.

One day the elephant took her calves to a water hole she knew. But when they arrived, there was only dry, cracked earth. The elephant scraped at the ground. She could smell water and she knew there must be some still under the ground. So she dug down and down with her tusks. The calves watched as she worked. Then, slowly the hole she had dug filled with cool clear water. The elephant lowered her trunk into the hole, sucked up the water and squirted it into her dry mouth. Then her calves had a drink.

The elephants drank as much as their bellies could hold. Then they trudged off to find food.

As they went, a giraffe came striding out from behind the trees, to steal a drink from the elephant's hole. But just as it was about to drink, the younger calf came back.

The giraffe hurriedly tried to get up and run away. Its long legs got tangled up and its neck waved wildly from side to side as it tried to scramble to its feet. The calf waited until the frightened thief had gone, and then sucked up some water to wash her hot skin.

The calf sprayed herself with water from the hole and stood waiting for it to fill up again. She did not know that a hungry lion had smelled the water and was lurking nearby. The lion crept closer, so quietly that the little elephant did not hear it. But the egrets, perching on the back of the calf's mother, sensed danger and flew away.

The mother turned and caught the lion's scent. She charged over to her calf and stood between her and the lion. She trumpeted fiercely and lowered her head to stab the lion with her tusks. The lion snarled and snapped as the

elephant charged towards it, head down. Then, afraid of the sharp tusks, the lion turned and headed back to the bushes.

The little elephant was not hurt, but she was trembling with fright. She stayed close to her mother for a long time after that.

All this time a baby had been growing inside the elephant. She had been carrying the baby for almost two years. Now it was time for her to give birth.

When she was ready to have the baby she stole away to a secret place. Two older females plodded after her. They had calves of their own and could help with the new baby.

After the baby was born, the elephant rested. Her friends licked the tiny animal all over. Then, curling their trunks under his belly, they lifted him gently to his feet. But his knees were wobbly and he could only stand for a moment before he flopped to the ground. They prodded him softly and nudged him with their trunks until he was on his feet again.

Soon he could stand and suck the warm milk from his mother. He had to curl his trunk backwards so that it would not get in the way.

After two days the calf could follow the herd. He was still unsteady on his feet and sometimes he was so tired that his little legs ached. But he had to keep up. If he were left behind he would be easy prey for hungry lions or wild dogs.

Although the other members of the herd were friendly, the mother elephant never let her calf stray from her side. He was too small to play with the older calves. Their games were too rough for him. He had not even learned how to use his trunk yet.

The elephant took special care not to let her oldest calf near the baby. The male calf was bigger and rougher than all the others, and often fought with the other young males in the herd.

One day, he got angry with his sister and charged at her. She was badly cut and one of her tusks was broken off. It was time for him to leave the herd. He was too old to stay with the other calves.

The older elephants drove him away and would not let him rejoin the herd. He followed them for a few days, squealing to his mother, but she took no notice. So he went off with two other young males who had been following the herd. Later he might find a mate from another herd.

At the end of the dry season, huge, grey clouds gathered over the plains and there was a taste of rain in the air. One evening, big drops began to splatter on the burnt grass. The elephant stood in the rain, flapping her ears and trumpeting loudly. Now there would be enough water for drinking and bathing. Her calves ran around her, splashing their big feet in the puddles and squirting each other with water. It was the first rain that the baby elephant had ever seen.

The dry water holes and river beds filled with water. New green grass sprang up between the old brown stems, and soon fresh, tasty food was everywhere. The elephant and her calves would not have to travel so far to find food and water. They could stay near their favourite water hole until the weather changed and it was time for them to start their travels again.

Elephant Facts

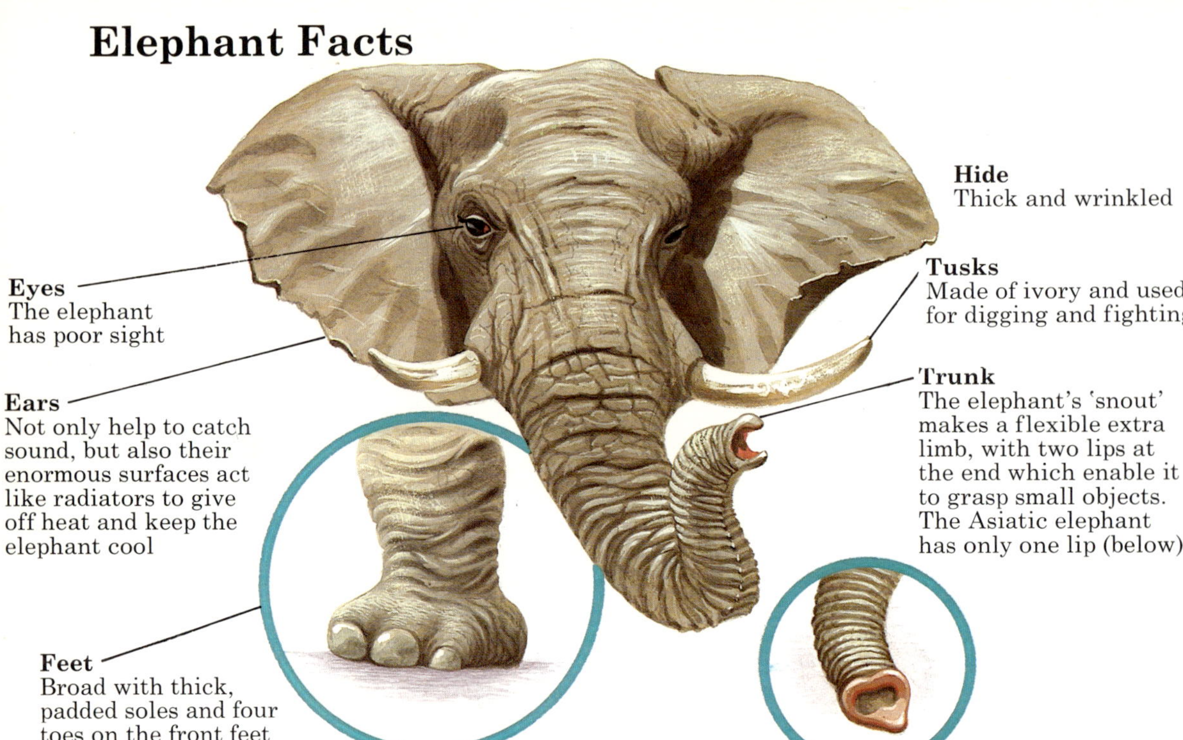

The head of an African elephant

There are two main types of elephant. The African elephant in the story lives in most parts of Africa, south of the Sahara desert. The Asiatic (Indian) elephant lives in India and most parts of South East Asia.

Big Ears or Small

The African elephant is larger than the Asiatic. It is up to 3·5 metres high and weighs up to six tonnes. It has bigger ears and tusks than its cousin and two 'lips' at the end of its trunk rather than one. Its big ears help to keep it cool, so it can live on the hot plains. The Asiatic elephant needs more shade and lives mainly in the jungle.

The elephant's trunk is a nose and an arm all in one. By lifting it and sniffing the air, the elephant can smell water or other animals from a long way away. It can also use its trunk like an arm to grasp leaves and grass, and like a straw to suck up water for drinking and taking a shower. The trunk can hold over four litres of water.

As well as showers, elephants like dust baths to brush away pests from their skin. They suck up the dry dust and blow it over their backs.

Though the trunk is strong enough to lift up whole trees, the 'lips' at the end of it are so gentle that the elephant can pick delicate berries.

The elephant also has surprisingly sensitive feet. Despite a layer of thick skin on the broad soles, the flexible toes allow it to move quietly and to climb rocky slopes without slipping. Its pillar-like legs provide support for its massive weight.

Tusks and Teeth

Elephants spend about 16 hours or more each day simply feeding. They eat up to 300 kilograms of greenery each day and every mouthful has to be chewed. Fortunately the elephant's broad, flat cheek teeth are replaced when they wear out. When the last set – it has six in a lifetime – wears out, the elephant dies because it can no longer grind up its food. One set of teeth that do not grow again are the elephant's tusks. These are really overgrown front teeth.

The tusks are made of ivory, a highly valued substance. Ivory hunters have killed so many elephants that now the animals are mostly kept in game parks where they can be protected.

Elephants at Work

As early as 1500 BC, elephants were trained to work for men and carry them in battle. Nowadays, elephants work mainly in forests, pulling down trees and dragging logs into piles. They are captured in the jungle and then tied to a tame elephant, or 'koonkie'. The 'koonkie' helps the elephant trainer, or 'mahout', to teach the new elephant what to do. It is mainly Asiatic elephants that do this kind of work.

J. Allen Cash Ltd

With no sign of effort, a young Asiatic elephant carries its equally young 'mahout' and a log.

Tall Stories

The first Europeans to explore inner Africa brought back tales of 'elephant graveyards', special places where elephants go to die. These stories may not have been true, but people have since seen elephants gathering round a dying member of the herd, touching it with their trunks and putting leaves on its head. They have also been seen to cover the bodies of dead elephants with leaves and branches.

Many people say that 'an elephant never forgets'. Elephants are intelligent and, although they do not have perfect memories, they can be trained to do difficult tasks.

More books for you to read from
ANGUS & ROBERTSON

WILDLIFE LIBRARY

If you have enjoyed this book, you will be pleased to know that it is part of a series:

The Tiger
0 207 95819 X

The Kangaroo
0 207 95820 3

The Penguin
0 207 95821 1

The Beaver
0 207 95822 X

The Wolf
0 207 95843 2

The Bear
0 207 95844 0

The Elephant
0 207 95845 9

The Deer
0 207 95846 7

EYE-VIEW LIBRARY

In addition, there are ten titles in the Eye-View Library, a companion series about the smaller creatures of the countryside:

The Song Thrush
0 207 95695 2

The Hedgehog
0 207 95693 6

The Bumblebee
0 207 95694 4

The Squirrel
0 207 95710 X

The Frog
0 207 95708 8

The Butterfly
0 207 95709 6

The Fox
0 207 95772 X

The Mouse
0 207 95773 8

The Duck
0 207 95832 7

The Otter
0 207 95833 5

All the books are in full colour.